ISBN: 9798871217139

CONTENTS

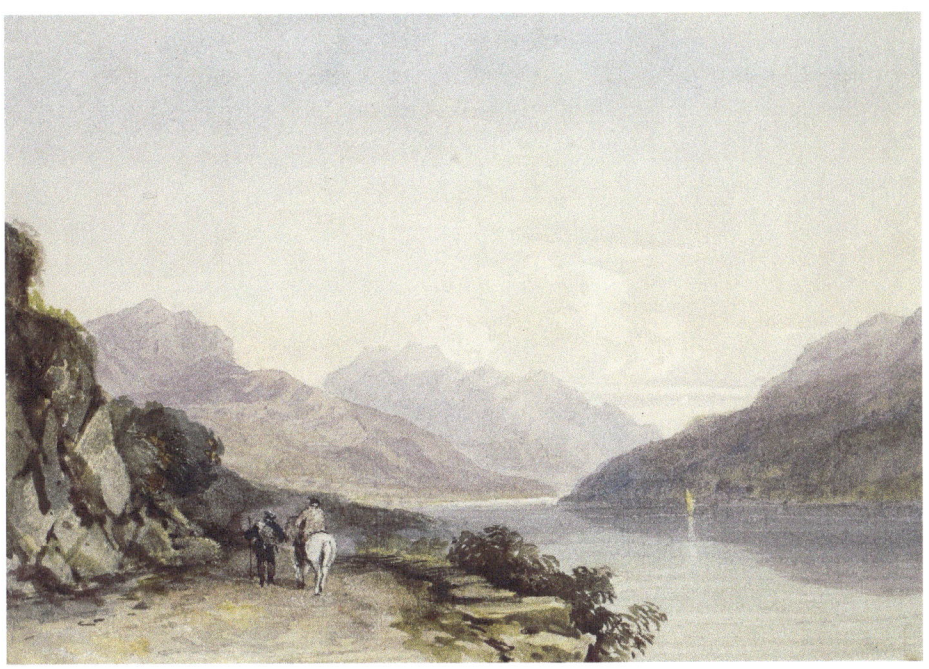

'The Path By The Lake', Ben Voirlich, 1836 by David Cox Junior

YOUR ARTISTIC ODYSSEY BEGINS.

In a world dominated by colors, strokes, and unbridled creativity, the allure of a career in art stands as a magnetic force, beckoning those ready to transform passion into profession. Welcome to the gritty yet enchanting world of "Artful Ambitions: Your Path to a Thriving Art Career."

This isn't a journey for the faint-hearted. It's a practical exploration into the dynamics of building a sustainable career from your artistic prowess. As we embark on this expedition, we won't just romanticize the canvas; we'll delve into the nuts and bolts of honing your skills, crafting a compelling body of work, and navigating the digital landscape.

So, what's the draw? What makes the pursuit of art a compelling choice? This book cuts through the sentimentality to provide a pragmatic overview of the road ahead. It's about mastering your craft, strategically presenting your work, and understanding the nuances of an art career that extends beyond traditional boundaries.

Consider this not just a guide but a roadmap—a roadmap that dissects the intricacies of turning your passion into a thriving career. Whether you're a brush-wielding traditionalist or a digital virtuoso, the journey is about to begin. Buckle up; your artistic odyssey awaits.

CHAPTER 2: MASTERING SKILLS

In the intricate dance between imagination and manifestation, mastering artistic skills becomes the cornerstone of success. In this chapter, we'll delve into the essentials of honing your craft, emphasizing the significance of continuous learning, discovering your unique artistic voice, and striking the delicate balance between traditional and contemporary skills.

The Foundation of Artistic Success

At the heart of every masterpiece lies a foundation built on skill. Consider the great artists of history—Leonardo da Vinci, Vincent van Gogh, or Frida Kahlo. Their brilliance wasn't solely born from inspiration; it was forged through a meticulous dedication to honing their craft. This dedication is the essence of the artistic journey.

Crafting your skills requires a commitment to practice. Much like an athlete perfects their form or a musician refines their technique, an artist sharpens their abilities through consistent, purposeful practice. Whether it's sketching, painting, sculpting, or mastering digital tools, the act of creation becomes a ritual that shapes raw talent into refined expertise.

Importance of Continuous Learning

Artistic growth thrives on a fertile ground of perpetual learning. The creative world evolves, and so must the artist. Embrace a mindset of continuous improvement. Attend workshops, enroll in courses, and seek mentorship. The more diverse your sources of learning, the richer your artistic palette becomes.

The digital age has brought forth an abundance of resources, making learning more accessible than ever. Online platforms offer tutorials, masterclasses, and communities where artists share insights and critiques. Be an active participant in this exchange of knowledge and watch your skills flourish in the dynamic landscape of artistic evolution.

Identifying and Honing Your Unique Style

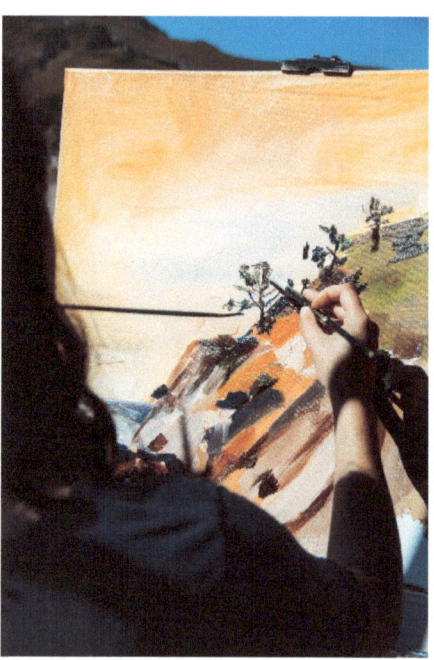

In a world teeming with artistic expressions, finding your unique voice is a journey of self-discovery. What themes resonate with you? What emotions do you wish to convey through your work? These questions guide you toward your artistic identity.

Your style is not merely a technique; it's a reflection of your perspective, your interpretation of the world. Analyse your favourite works of art, explore various genres, and experiment with different mediums. Your style emerges not from imitation but from a fusion of influences, gradually transforming into a signature that sets your work apart.

Balancing Traditional and Contemporary Skills

Artistry, like any craft, is a delicate balance between tradition and innovation. Traditional skills form the backbone, providing a solid framework for your artistic endeavours. Whether it's mastering classical painting techniques or understanding the principles of composition, these foundations empower you to push creative boundaries.

However, the contemporary artist must also embrace the tools of the present and future. Digital platforms, graphic design software, and virtual reality are not adversaries but allies in your artistic arsenal. The ability to seamlessly navigate between traditional and contemporary skills opens new avenues for expression and expands your reach in an ever-evolving art landscape.

Striking this balance is an ongoing process. It's about respecting the roots of artistic expression while fearlessly exploring the uncharted territories of modern creativity. The fusion of these elements not only enhances your versatility but also positions you at the forefront of artistic innovation.

The Evolution Begins

As you immerse yourself in the journey of mastering skills, remember that it's not a sprint but a marathon. The foundation you lay today becomes the platform for tomorrow's artistic triumphs. Craft. Create. Elevate. These are not just words; they're a mantra for every artist seeking not just success but mastery in their chosen craft.

In the next chapters, we'll build upon this foundation, exploring how to translate your honed skills into a compelling body of work and navigate the intricacies of a digital landscape that both challenges and propels the modern artist. Your evolution as an artist has begun; embrace the canvas of possibilities that lies ahead.

CHAPTER 3: PORTFOLIO POWER: BUILDING YOUR BODY OF WORK

In the competitive realm of art, your portfolio is not just a collection of pieces; it is your artistic signature, a visual narrative that communicates your unique voice to the world. In this chapter, we will explore the intricacies of crafting a compelling portfolio, selecting, and organizing your best pieces, the importance of diversity in your body of work, and the dynamic evolution of an artist's portfolio over time.

Crafting a Compelling Portfolio

Think of your portfolio as your artistic showcase—a carefully curated exhibit that invites viewers into the realm of your creativity. Crafting a compelling portfolio involves a blend of strategic selection and storytelling. Begin by defining the purpose of your portfolio. Is it intended for gallery submissions, online platforms, or potential clients? Tailor your selection to align with your goals.

Consider the narrative flow. Your portfolio should tell a story, capturing the evolution of your skills and the thematic threads that run through your work. Start with a captivating piece that grabs attention, then guide the viewer through a visual journey that reflects the depth and breadth of your artistic prowess.

Selecting and Organizing Your Best Pieces

Quality over quantity is the mantra when selecting pieces for your portfolio. Each artwork should be a testament to your skill, creativity, and the message you wish to convey. Be discerning—include pieces that not only showcase technical proficiency but also resonate with your artistic identity.

Organize your portfolio with intention. Group similar works together to create visual coherence. Consider the flow of colors, themes, or mediums to maintain a harmonious rhythm.

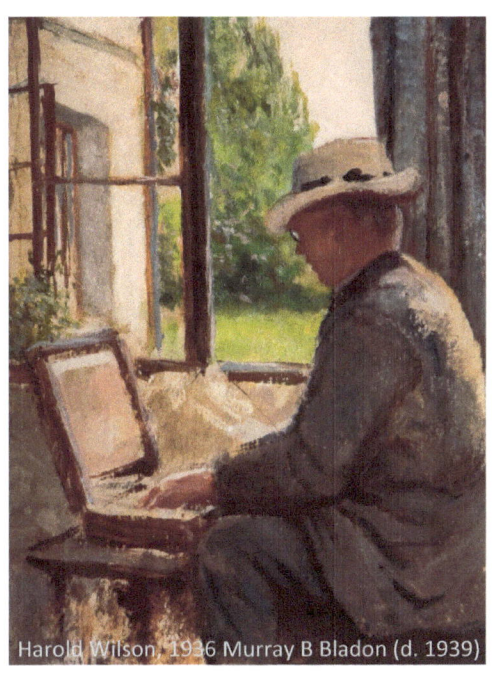
Harold Wilson, 1936 Murray B Bladon (d. 1939)

A well-organized portfolio not only enhances the viewer's experience but also reflects your attention to detail and professionalism.

Incorporating Diversity in Your Body of Work

Diversity in your portfolio is not just about showcasing a range of subjects; it's a demonstration of your adaptability and creative versatility. Explore different styles, mediums, and themes to showcase the depth of your artistic palette. A diverse portfolio not only captures a wider audience but also positions you as an artist capable of navigating various artistic landscapes.

However, don't sacrifice cohesion for diversity. While variety is essential, ensure that there's a unifying thread that ties your diverse pieces together. Whether it's a recurring motif, a consistent colour palette, or a thematic undercurrent, find the balance between variety and coherence.

The Evolution of an Artist's Portfolio

An artist's portfolio is not a static entity; it is a living, breathing testament to your growth and evolution. As you progress in your artistic journey, revisit and refresh your portfolio regularly. Remove pieces that no longer align with your current style or vision, making space for newer, more representative works.

Consider your portfolio as a dynamic entity that evolves with you. Your early works may showcase raw talent and experimentation, while later pieces reflect a refined and matured artistic voice. Embrace this evolution and let your portfolio serve as a visual timeline of your artistic odyssey.

Your Visual Legacy

Your portfolio is more than a compilation of artworks; it is your visual legacy. Crafting it requires a keen understanding of your artistic identity, a discerning eye for selection, and the willingness to embrace the ever-changing nature of your craft.

As you embark on this journey of building your body of work, remember that your portfolio is not set in stone. It is a canvas waiting for your next stroke, your next masterpiece. In the chapters ahead, we'll explore how to capture the essence of your artwork through the lens and unveil the digital realm's potential in showcasing your portfolio to a global audience. Your visual legacy awaits—craft it with intention, passion, and the ever-present spirit of innovation.

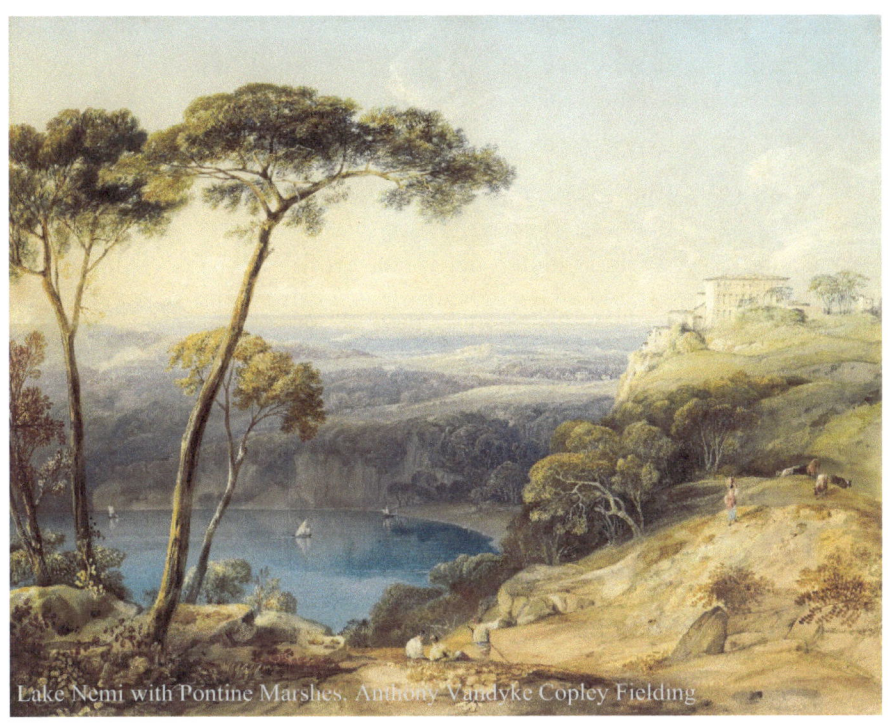

Lake Nemi with Pontine Marshes, Anthony Vandyke Copley Fielding

CHAPTER 4: PICTURE-PERFECT: PHOTOGRAPHING YOUR ARTWORK

In the digital age, the lens has become an artist's ally, transforming physical masterpieces into virtual treasures accessible to a global audience. This chapter delves into the art of capturing your artwork through the lens, exploring the significance of high-quality images, setting up a budget-friendly home studio, mastering lighting and angles, and the strategic use of post-processing tools for optimal results.

The Significance of High-Quality Images

Your artwork deserves to be seen in its full glory, and the gateway to a viewer's appreciation is through high-quality images. The significance of this step cannot be overstated. In the vast expanse of the internet and the competitive world of art, an image is often the first and lasting impression.

Invest time in capturing your artwork with a camera that can render details accurately. Whether you use a DSLR, mirrorless camera, or even a high-end smartphone, the key is to ensure that the final image does justice to the nuances of your creation. A crisp, well-lit image not only showcases your skill but also invites viewers into the intricate details and textures of your work.

Setting Up a Budget-Friendly Home Studio

Creating a makeshift studio need not break the bank. With a few budget-friendly tools and a bit of creativity, you can establish a home studio that elevates the presentation of your artwork. Begin by selecting a dedicated space with ample natural light. If that's not feasible, invest in soft, diffused lighting to minimize harsh shadows.

A neutral backdrop, be it a white wall or a large sheet of paper, ensures that your artwork takes centre stage without distractions. Experiment with different angles and arrangements until you find a setup that complements your artistic vision. Remember, simplicity often enhances the visual impact.

Mastering Lighting and Angles

Lighting is the maestro that orchestrates the visual symphony of your artwork. Natural light is a powerful ally, offering a balanced and true-to-life representation of colors and textures. Position your artwork so that it receives even illumination, avoiding harsh shadows that can obscure details.

If natural light is limited, artificial lighting can be an effective alternative. Invest in softboxes or diffusers to create a gentle, uniform glow. Experiment with the positioning of lights to minimize reflections and capture the essence of your artwork authentically.

Angles play a pivotal role in how your artwork is perceived. A straight-on shot provides a faithful representation, while experimenting with angles can add depth and dimension. Consider capturing close-ups to highlight intricate details or opt for a broader view to showcase the entirety of larger pieces. The goal is to present your artwork in a way that engages the viewer and conveys your artistic intent.

Utilizing Post-Processing Tools for Optimal Results

Once the images are captured, the journey doesn't end there. Post-processing is the final brushstroke that refines your digital representation. While the goal is authenticity, subtle enhancements can elevate the visual impact. Consider investing time in learning basic editing techniques or enlist the help of user-friendly software.

Adjusting contrast, brightness, and colour balance can fine-tune your image, ensuring it aligns with the true essence of your artwork. Be cautious not to over-process; the aim is to enhance, not alter. Additionally, cropping can be a powerful tool to focus attention on specific details or to achieve a balanced composition.

A Visual Symphony Unveiled

In the realm of digital presentation, your artwork's portrayal is as significant as the creation itself. The art of photographing your artwork is a skill worth mastering—a skill that bridges the tangible and virtual, inviting a global audience into your creative universe.

As you embark on capturing your artistic creations through the lens, remember that each click is an opportunity to communicate your artistic voice. In the chapters ahead, we'll explore avenues to showcase your portfolio online and strategies to navigate the digital landscape seamlessly. Your visual symphony is ready to be unveiled—let the camera be your conductor in this captivating journey of artistry.

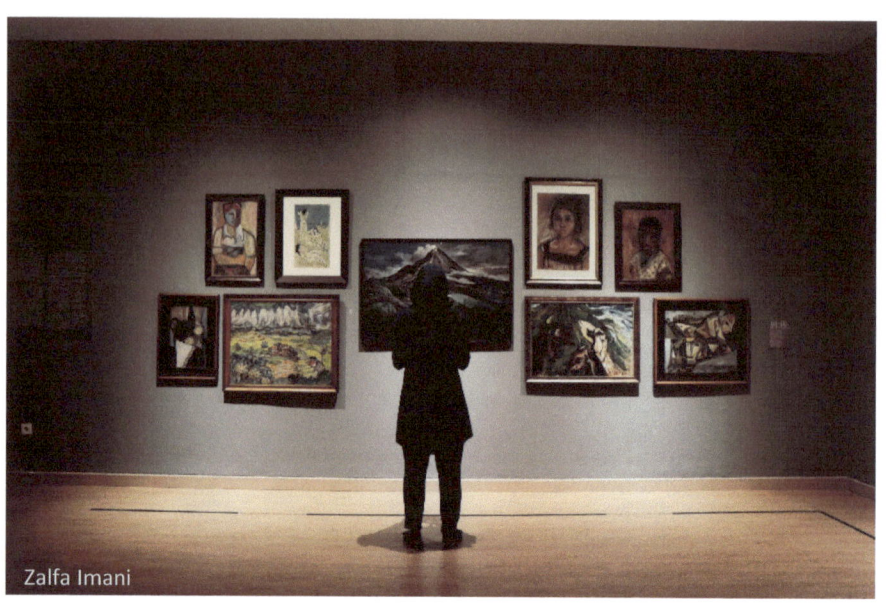

Zalfa Imani

CHAPTER 5: DIGITAL MASTERY: ESTABLISHING YOUR ART DATABASE

In the age of pixels and screens, the organization and management of your artistic endeavours demand a digital evolution. This chapter unfolds the realm of digital mastery, guiding you through the process of organizing and categorizing your work digitally, selecting the right database software, implementing robust backup strategies, and seamlessly integrating database management into your creative routine.

Organizing and Categorizing Your Work Digitally

A digital art database is more than a storage facility; it's a dynamic archive that breathes life into your creative journey. Start by organizing your work systematically. Create folders that reflect different aspects of your artistic journey, such as genres, themes, or mediums. This meticulous categorization will not only make retrieving specific pieces a breeze but also provide insights into the evolution of your style over time.

Consider using a naming convention that is both intuitive and consistent. Whether it's date-based, thematic, or a combination of both, a well-structured naming system ensures that each file is a puzzle piece that fits seamlessly into the larger picture of your artistic narrative.

Selecting the Right Database Software

Choosing the right database software is akin to selecting the perfect brush for a painting—it shapes the outcome and influences the entire creative process. Several options cater specifically to artists, offering features tailored to the nuances of visual content organization.

Consider platforms like Adobe Lightroom, Artwork Archive, or even a customized solution using platforms like Airtable or Google Sheets. The choice depends on your specific needs, budget constraints, and the level of customization required. Experiment with different options to find the software that aligns seamlessly with your workflow.

The selected software should allow for not only easy categorization but also the addition of metadata. Tagging each artwork with relevant information, such as creation date, dimensions, and the inspiration behind it, transforms your database into a rich source of contextual information.

Backing Up Your Artistic Endeavours

In the digital realm, where the unforeseen is a constant companion, the importance of backing up your artistic endeavours cannot be overstated. Consider your art database not just as a collection of files but as a vault safeguarding your creative legacy. Regular backups are the keys to this vault, ensuring that no stroke, colour, or concept is lost to the digital void.

Cloud-based storage solutions like Google Drive, Dropbox, or dedicated art management platforms often offer seamless backup options. Establish a routine—whether it's weekly or monthly—to update your backup. This not only protects against potential data loss but also instills peace of mind, allowing you to focus on your creative process without the looming threat of digital mishaps.

Integrating Database Management into Your Routine

A well-organized digital database becomes a creative ally when seamlessly integrated into your routine. Treat the management of your digital archive as an ongoing practice rather than a sporadic task. Dedicate time regularly to update new pieces, tweak metadata, and ensure that your database reflects the current state of your artistic journey.

Consider establishing a naming and filing ritual for each new creation.

This not only streamlines the digital filing process but also reinforces the habit of maintaining an organized database. Embrace the digital management routine as an integral part of your creative discipline—it's an investment that pays dividends in the efficiency and clarity of your artistic process.

Pixels to Prosperity

In the digital era, where every pixel holds the potential for prosperity, the establishment of an art database is not a mere technicality but a strategic move toward artistic empowerment. From the organization of files to the selection of the right software, and the implementation of robust backup strategies, each step is a pixel contributing to the larger picture of your success.

As you embark on this journey from pixels to prosperity, consider your digital database not just as a storage solution but as a dynamic tool that fuels your artistic evolution, as not only does a smooth system provide you an objective overview of your work, but it also creates a professional and efficient impression to possible collaborators. In the upcoming chapters, we'll explore avenues to transform your digital assets into a powerful online presence, ensuring that your art resonates with a global audience. Let the pixels be the building blocks of your artistic empire, where organization meets innovation, and prosperity awaits.

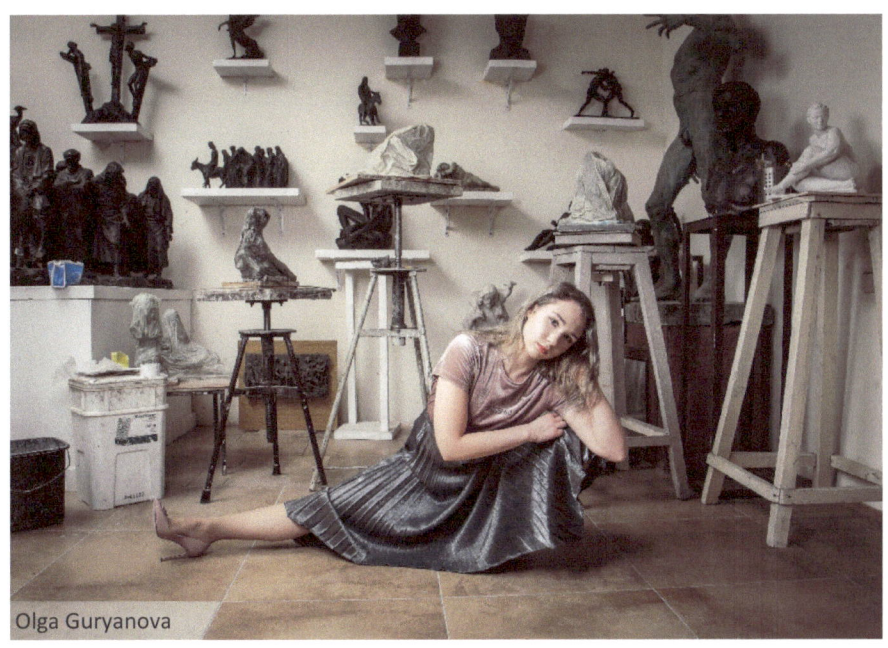
Olga Guryanova

CHAPTER 6: CRAFT YOUR CANVAS: BUILDING AN ARTIST'S RESUME

In the competitive landscape of the art world, your resume is more than a list of achievements; it is a canvas that paints a picture of your artistic journey, showcasing the skills, experiences, and nuances that define you as an artist. This chapter delves into the nuances of crafting an artist's resume—a crucial tool that extends your artistry beyond the easel. We'll explore the art of highlighting relevant experiences, tailoring your resume for diverse opportunities, and striking the delicate balance between humility and self-promotion.

The Artistic Resume: A Crucial Tool

Think of your artistic resume as a curated exhibition of your professional journey. It's not merely a list of past roles or accolades; it's a visual narrative that communicates your artistic identity. Begin with a concise and compelling artist statement—an introduction that captures the essence of your work, your inspirations, and your artistic philosophy.

Beyond the standard details like your contact information and educational background, your resume should include a section dedicated to exhibitions, both solo and group. List any awards, honours, or residencies you've garnered, showcasing the external validation of your artistic merit. Include relevant skills, from technical proficiencies to languages spoken, providing a comprehensive view of your capabilities.

Highlighting Relevant Experiences and Achievements

When building your artistic resume, prioritize experiences and achievements that align with your artistic vision and the opportunities you seek. If you've participated in exhibitions, specify the venues and dates. Highlight any awards or recognitions, emphasizing how they contribute to the narrative of your artistic journey.

Consider including any collaborations, whether with other artists, galleries, or community projects. These collaborations not only showcase your ability to work within a creative ecosystem but also demonstrate your commitment to the broader artistic community. Include any publications, articles, or features where your work has been showcased, underscoring your presence in the art world.

Tailoring Your Resume for Different Opportunities

One size does not fit all when it comes to an artist's resume. Tailor your document for each opportunity, aligning your experiences and achievements with the specific requirements or themes of the opportunity at hand. If you're applying for a residency, emphasize your previous residency experiences. For a gallery submission, focus on relevant exhibitions and your unique artistic perspective.

Consider creating different versions of your resume to cater to diverse opportunities. This customization not only showcases your attention to detail but also positions you as an artist who tailors their approach to suit the specific demands of each opportunity.

Balancing Humility and Self-Promotion

Crafting an artist's resume involves striking a delicate balance between humility and self-promotion. While it's crucial to showcase your achievements and skills, avoid veering into the realm of arrogance. Let your work speak for itself, and let your resume serve as a modest guide that allows viewers to navigate your artistic journey.

When highlighting experiences, focus on the impact and growth rather than merely listing accomplishments. Use language that reflects your passion for your craft and your dedication to continuous improvement. Humility doesn't diminish your achievements; it adds authenticity and relatability to your artistic narrative.

Your Resume, Your Artistic Canvas

Your artist's resume is not a static document but a dynamic canvas that evolves with each stroke of your artistic journey. Approach it with the same creativity and attention to detail that you apply to your artwork. Craft it as an extension of your artistic identity, a visual representation of the path you've travelled and the destinations you aspire to reach.

As we move forward, we'll explore avenues to showcase your resume digitally, leveraging online platforms to maximize its impact. Your resume is not just a record; it's an invitation for others to join you on your artistic expedition. Let it be a testament to your journey, an embodiment of your artistic essence beyond the easel. The canvas is yours; paint it with the strokes of your artistic narrative.

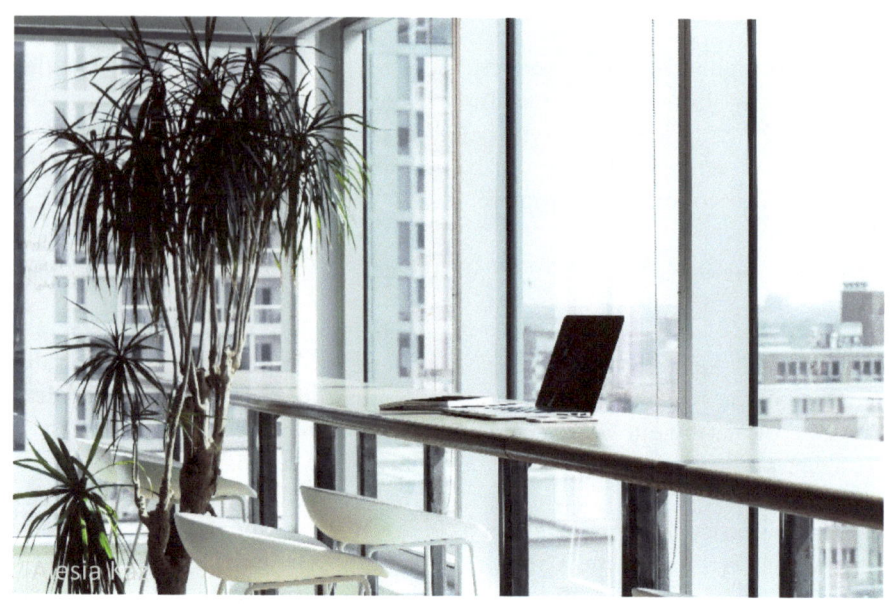

CHAPTER 7: ART MARKET ALCHEMY: SELLING YOUR MASTERPIECES ONLINE

In the digital age, the art market is no longer confined to brick-and-mortar galleries; it's a vast online landscape where artists can turn clicks into canvases. This chapter delves into the intricacies of selling your masterpieces online—an alchemical process that requires navigating various platforms, crafting an effective artist profile, setting prices with an understanding of the market, and mastering the art of managing sales and customer interactions.

Navigating Online Platforms

The online art market is a bustling marketplace with a multitude of platforms vying for attention. Whether you're a seasoned artist or just starting, selecting the right platform is pivotal. Each platform has its unique audience, policies, and fee structures.

Consider renowned platforms like Etsy, Saatchi Art, or Art finder for a diverse audience and straightforward setup. If you're venturing into the digital art realm, platforms like Redbubble or Society6 cater to print-on-demand services. Social media platforms, particularly Instagram and

Facebook, also provide avenues to showcase and sell your art directly.

Research and choose platforms aligning with your artistic style, target audience, and long-term goals. Each platform has its own nuances, so take the time to familiarize yourself with their features, policies, and community dynamics.

Platform Evaluation Examples:

1. **Etsy:**
   - Ideal for artists creating unique, handcrafted pieces.
   - Appeals to a diverse audience seeking original and personalized artworks.
   - Offers a straightforward setup process and a built-in customer base interested in supporting independent artists.
2. **Saatchi Art:**
   - Targets a global audience with a focus on emerging artists.
   - Provides exposure through curated collections and online exhibitions.
   - Allows artists to set their prices and keep a majority of the sales revenue.
3. **Artfinder:**
   - Emphasizes a curated selection of artworks, connecting buyers with independent artists.
   - Incorporates a discovery algorithm, exposing artists to potential buyers based on their preferences.
   - Offers a user-friendly interface for artists to manage their online presence and sales.
4. **Redbubble and Society6:**
   - Tailored for digital artists and creators of print-on-demand products.
   - Enables artists to showcase their work on various products like prints, clothing, and accessories.
   - Simplifies the production and shipping process, allowing artists to focus on creating.
5. **Instagram and Facebook:**
   - Social media platforms where artists can directly showcase and sell their work.
   - Utilize features like Instagram Shops or Facebook Marketplace for seamless transactions.
   - Leverage hashtags, stories, and posts to engage with a broader audience.

Each platform has its strengths, and the key is to align your artistic style and goals with the platform that best suits your needs. Experiment with a combination of platforms to diversify your online presence and maximize your reach.

Creating an Effective Artist Profile

Your artist profile is your digital storefront—a space where potential buyers get a glimpse into your artistic universe. Invest time in crafting a profile that not only showcases your artwork but also communicates your artistic story. Use a captivating bio that reflects your inspiration, journey, and the essence of your work.

Key Elements of an Effective Artistic Profile:

1. **Compelling Bio:**
   - Communicate your artistic journey, inspirations, and philosophy.
   - Offer a glimpse into the person behind the art, fostering a personal connection.
2. **Visual Showcase:**
   - Display a range of your best pieces to provide a comprehensive overview of your style.
   - Include behind-the-scenes glimpses to humanize your creative process.
3. **Accomplishments and Collaborations:**
   - Highlight exhibitions, awards, or features to showcase external validation.
   - Include any collaborations to emphasize your participation in the broader artistic community.

Setting Prices and Understanding the Market

Pricing your artwork strategically requires a delicate balance between recognizing your artistic worth and understanding market dynamics.

1. Research Comparable Works:

Explore platforms to understand pricing trends for artists with similar styles and experience levels. Consider factors like size, medium, and time invested in each piece.

2. Factor in Value:

Avoid undervaluing your work; consider material costs, time spent, and the unique qualities of your art. Many new artists feel the need to start off pricing their art low, but this may result in people viewing your art as low value. Consider whether your priority is being a lower value artist selling lots of work, or a higher value artist selling less work for higher prices. Keep in mind that pricing = value = your brand image.

If you're offering limited editions or prints, clearly communicate the exclusivity and value associated with these pieces. This transparency builds trust with potential buyers and positions your art within the broader market context.

   3.   Consistent Pricing:
Maintain a consistent pricing strategy across platforms to build credibility. Ensure transparency about your pricing approach to instil trust in potential buyers.

Marketing, Advertising, and Promotion

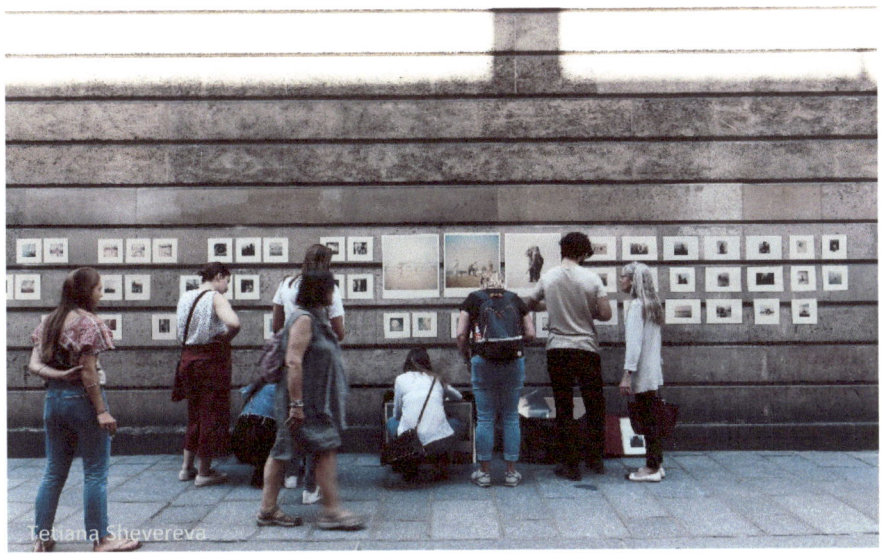

Beyond selecting the right platform, actively marketing, advertising, and promoting your art are integral components of online success.

1. **Social Media Engagement:**
    - Leverage the power of social media to reach a wider

audience.

- Share regular updates, engage with followers, contact art promotion accounts, and use relevant hashtags to increase visibility.

2. **Email Marketing:**
   - Build an email list of interested buyers and art enthusiasts.
   - Send regular newsletters showcasing new works, upcoming exhibitions, or exclusive promotions.

3. **Collaborations and Cross-Promotions:**
   - Collaborate with other artists or influencers for cross-promotions.
   - Participate in virtual art events or online exhibitions to broaden your reach.

4. **Optimized Website:**
   - If you have a personal website, ensure it is optimized for search engines (SEO).
   - Regularly update it with new pieces, blog posts, or insights into your artistic process.

5. **Paid Advertising:**
   - Consider targeted paid advertising on platforms like Facebook or Instagram to reach specific demographics.
   - Monitor and analyse the performance of your ads to refine your approach.

Managing Sales and Customer Interactions

Once the clicks start converting into sales, effective management becomes key (this is also where your efficient organisation system we discussed earlier comes in handy). Promptly respond to inquiries and engage with potential buyers. Clear communication builds trust and enhances the overall buying experience.

Packaging and shipping are extensions of your artistic brand. Ensure that your artwork is securely packaged to prevent damage during transit. Include a personal touch, such as a thank-you note or a small token of appreciation. This attention to detail transforms a transaction into a memorable interaction, increasing the likelihood of repeat business or positive reviews.

Embrace feedback, both positive and constructive. Feedback is not just a measure of customer satisfaction; it's a tool for continuous improvement. If a customer expresses concern, address it promptly and professionally. Your approach to customer interactions contributes to your reputation as an artist, impacting not only sales but also the growth of your artistic brand.

From Clicks to Canvases, A Digital Artistry Journey

Selling your masterpieces online is not just about transactions; it's a nuanced journey that requires a strategic blend of platform selection, effective profile creation, pricing acumen, and dynamic marketing efforts.

As we progress, we'll delve deeper into finding your niche in the art market, dispelling misconceptions and romanticisms, and the variety of careers available to you in this industry. advanced strategies for promoting your art online, harnessing the potential of online communities, and building a brand that resonates globally. The digital canvas is expansive, and your mastery of online sales transforms it into a space where art and commerce seamlessly converge.

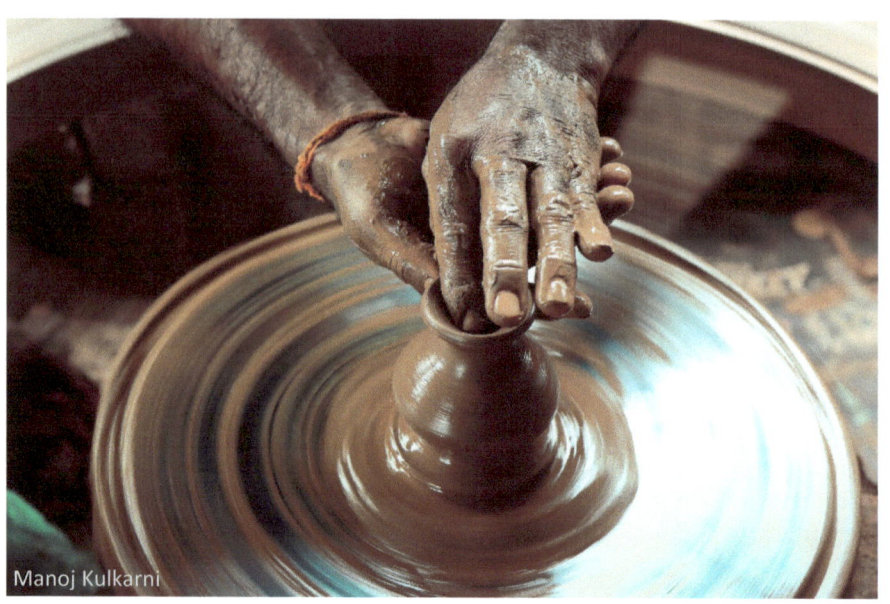
Manoj Kulkarni

CHAPTER 8: DIVERSE PATHS: NAVIGATING ART CAREERS

The world of art is a vast and varied landscape, offering a multitude of career paths for those seeking to turn their passion into a profession. This chapter serves as a guide through the diverse avenues within the art world, helping you find your niche, whether it's in fine arts, digital design, sculpture, or beyond. We'll explore the pros and cons of different artistic paths and provide insights into transitioning between art careers, allowing you to carve your unique artistic destiny.

Finding Your Niche: Fine Arts, Digital Design, Sculpture, and More

Unveiling your artistic niche is an intimately personal and evolving journey. It requires a blend of introspection, exploration, and a willingness to embrace the unknown.

- Begin by identifying your strengths, preferences, and the aspects of art that genuinely ignite your passion.
- Experiment with various mediums, techniques, and styles to uncover where your skills and interests align.
- Maintain an open-minded approach, allowing unexpected paths

and opportunities to shape your artistic identity.

How to transition between art careers

Transitioning between art careers is a natural evolution in an artist's journey, a transformative process that invites adaptability, growth, and the redefinition of one's artistic trajectory. This phase is an exploration of new possibilities, a mosaic of experiences that contribute to the richness of an artist's narrative.

Engage in thorough self-assessment as you stand at the crossroads of your artistic path. Reflect deeply on your current skills, interests, and the aspects of your current career that bring fulfilment. Understand the unique nuances that define your artistic identity and the elements that you want to carry forward into the next chapter of your creative exploration.

Investigate potential career options with curiosity and an open mind. Attend workshops, engage in conversations with professionals in your desired field, and immerse yourself in the atmosphere of the artistic realms you're contemplating. Networking becomes a powerful tool during this transition, offering insights, advice, and perhaps even mentorship from those who have successfully navigated similar changes.

Acquire any additional skills or qualifications necessary for your desired path. Education, whether formal or self-directed, becomes a bridge that connects your current expertise with the demands of your evolving career. Embrace the opportunity to learn, to stretch your artistic capabilities, and to acquire the tools that will empower your transition.

Develop a comprehensive transition plan that outlines the necessary steps for a successful shift. This plan should not only include the practical aspects, such as acquiring new skills or building a portfolio for the new path, but also consider the emotional and financial aspects of this transition. What safety nets can you put in place? How can you manage the potential uncertainties that may accompany a career shift?

Connect with professionals who have successfully navigated career transitions. Seek guidance and insights from those who have walked a similar path, absorbing the wisdom they've gained through their experiences. Their stories can provide inspiration, practical advice, and perhaps a sense of reassurance as you embark on your own artistic journey.

Embrace the learning curve that accompanies a new career. Understand that every new beginning involves a period of adjustment and growth. Challenges are not roadblocks but stepping stones, guiding you toward a deeper understanding of your craft and a broader perspective on the artistic landscape.

Recognize these challenges as opportunities for growth and adaptability. Your artistic evolution is not a linear path; it's a dynamic, ever-changing landscape. Embrace the twists and turns, the moments of uncertainty, and the exhilaration of discovering new facets of your creative self.

In this transition, allow your artistic intuition to be your guiding force. Listen to the whispers of inspiration, trust your instincts, and be open to the unexpected. Each step is a brushstroke on the canvas of your evolving artistic narrative, a testament to your resilience, creativity, and the boundless potential that lies within you.

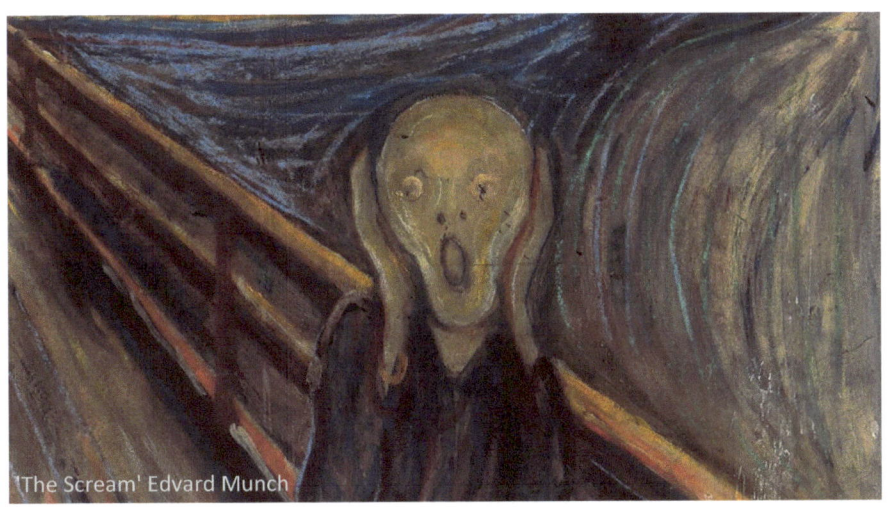
'The Scream' Edvard Munch

CHAPTER 9: ADDRESSING MISCONCEPTIONS ABOUT ART CAREERS

The allure of an art career often comes intertwined with romantic notions of the passionate artist, creating masterpieces in seclusion. Yet, navigating the path of an artist is more nuanced than the prevailing stereotypes suggest. In this chapter, we delve into the artistic realities, debunking the "starving artist" myth, exploring the pivotal role of business savvy in the art world, discussing the delicate balance between passion and practicality, and unravelling the complexities of realities versus romanticism in an art career.

Debunking the "Starving Artist" Myth

The image of the "starving artist" has persisted through centuries, perpetuating the notion that a successful art career is synonymous with financial struggle. However, this myth is not only outdated but also detrimental to emerging artists. The reality is that artists, like professionals in any field, can thrive and achieve financial stability with the right blend of talent, strategy, and resilience.

While it's true that establishing oneself in the art world requires dedication and perseverance, embracing the myth of destitution undermines the value of an artist's work. Acknowledging the potential for financial success allows emerging artists to approach their careers with a business mindset, setting the stage for a sustainable and prosperous journey.

The Role of Business Savvy in Art

Contrary to the romanticized image of the solitary artist solely driven by inspiration, successful artists today understand the vital role of business acumen in their careers. Beyond creating compelling artwork, navigating the art world necessitates a practical understanding of marketing, networking, and financial management.

Artists are not just creators; they are entrepreneurs shaping their brand and navigating the complex ecosystem of galleries, exhibitions, and online platforms. Establishing a successful art career involves treating art as both a passion and a business. This shift in perspective empowers artists to advocate for the value of their work, negotiate fair compensation, and strategically position themselves in the market.

The Balance Between Passion and Practicality

Passion fuels artistic endeavours, but the romantic notion of the tormented artist solely driven by their emotions often neglects the practical aspects of sustaining a career. Achieving a balance between passion and practicality is crucial for long-term success.

Artists must reconcile their creative visions with the demands of the market. This involves understanding the preferences of potential buyers, identifying trends, and sometimes adapting one's style to align with commercial viability. It's not a compromise of artistic integrity but rather a strategic approach to ensure that the passion for creation can be sustained over the course of a career.

Realities vs. Romanticism in an Art Career

The artistic journey is undeniably romanticized in popular culture. The idea of the bohemian artist, untethered by societal conventions, may seem appealing, but it often obscures the challenges artists face. Acknowledging the realities of an art career is not a betrayal of the romantic ideal; rather, it's a step towards a more informed and empowered artistic practice.

Realities include the need for self-promotion, the importance of a strong online presence, and the significance of professional networking. It involves navigating the administrative aspects of contracts, invoices, and client interactions. It's understanding that rejection is part of the artistic journey, and that resilience is as crucial as talent.

Embracing the Intersection of Passion and Pragmatism

The intersection of passion and pragmatism defines the modern artist's journey. It involves recognizing that artistic expression is not limited to the canvas; it extends to the way artists present and sustain their work in the world. Embracing this intersection allows artists to dismantle the "starving artist" myth and redefine success on their terms.

Thriving in the art world requires a multifaceted approach. It's about creating exceptional art while understanding the dynamics of the market. It's about nurturing the creative flame within while navigating the pragmatic landscapes of contracts and negotiations. This balance empowers artists to not only survive but to flourish in a landscape that rewards not only talent but also strategic thinking and resilience.

Breaking Free from Stereotypes

To break free from the shackles of stereotypes, emerging artists must embrace the duality of their roles. They are both creators and entrepreneurs, dreamers, and pragmatists. The canvas is not just a space for artistic expression but a platform for the artist to communicate their unique perspective to the world.

It's crucial to redefine success in the art world, moving beyond financial metrics to encompass artistic fulfilment, creative impact, and a sustained, thriving practice. Artists should resist the pressure to conform to outdated expectations and instead carve their own path, one that reflects their values, aspirations, and a holistic understanding of their craft.

In addressing misconceptions about art careers, emerging artists can forge a new narrative that celebrates the diverse and multifaceted nature of their profession. By embracing the intersection of passion and pragmatism, artists can create not only beautiful works of art but also sustainable, fulfilling, and impactful careers in the ever-evolving landscape of the art world.

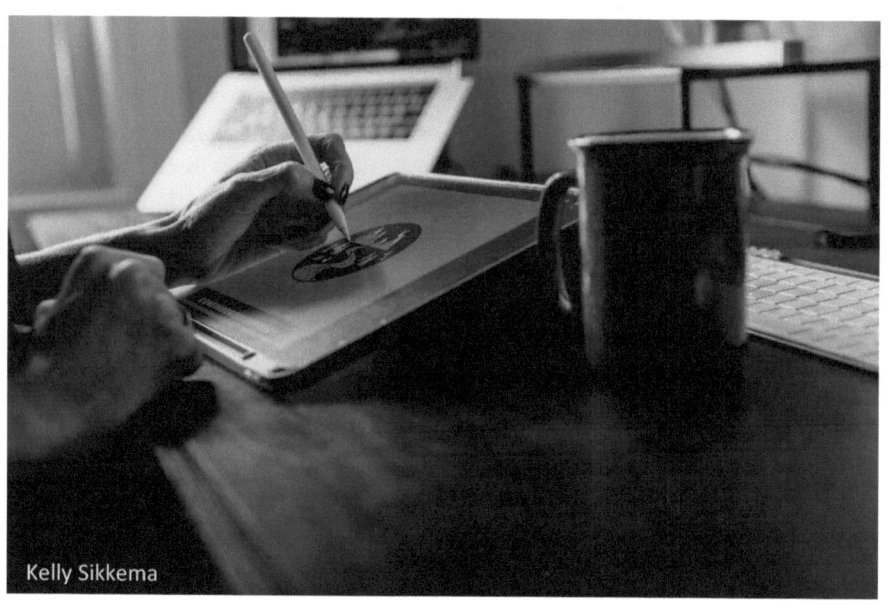
Kelly Sikkema

CHAPTER 10: BEYOND THE EASEL: A VARIETY OF ART-INFUSED CAREERS

The traditional image of an artist, solitary at an easel, is but one brushstroke on the expansive canvas of art careers. Beyond the confines of borders and canvases, a spectrum of art-infused professions beckons, each offering a unique avenue for creative expression. In this chapter, we explore an array of diverse paths, spanning Fine Arts, Sculpture, Art Therapy, Architecture, Graphic and Digital Design, Curating and Art Management, and the enriching realm of Teaching and Mentoring.

Fine Arts: Where the Canvas Knows No Bounds
Pros:
1. Freedom of Expression: Fine artists enjoy unparalleled freedom to express themselves without the constraints of commercial considerations.
2. Cultural Impact: Fine arts have the power to influence culture, challenging norms and sparking societal dialogue.
3. Versatility: Artists can explore various mediums, techniques, and styles, allowing for continuous evolution and experimentation.

Cons:
1. Financial Uncertainty: Success in the fine arts doesn't always

guarantee financial stability, leading to potential economic challenges.
2. Competitive Nature: The art world is highly competitive, requiring artists to navigate a crowded market for recognition and opportunities.
3. Subjectivity: Success in fine arts can be subjective, with personal taste and trends playing a significant role in an artist's recognition.

Sculpture: Shaping Dimensions into Existence
Pros:
1. Tactile Exploration: Sculptors engage in a hands-on exploration of materials, allowing for a unique and tactile artistic experience.
2. Public Interaction: Sculptures often invite physical interaction from the public, creating a dynamic relationship between the artwork and its audience.
3. Diverse Materials: Sculptors have the opportunity to work with a wide range of materials, from traditional stone to contemporary recycled materials.

Cons:
1. Physical Demands: Sculpting can be physically demanding, requiring endurance and the potential for strain or injury.
2. Logistical Challenges: Creating large-scale sculptures may involve logistical challenges, such as transportation and installation.
3. Niche Market: The market for sculptures can be niche, impacting the potential for widespread recognition and commercial success.

Art Therapy: Healing Through Creativity
Pros:
1. Emotional Impact: Art therapists witness the profound emotional impact of art on individuals, contributing to their healing and self-discovery.
2. Diverse Settings: Art therapists can work in various settings, including hospitals, schools, and community organizations, expanding their impact.
3. Personal Fulfilment: Helping others through creative expression can be deeply fulfilling for art therapists.

Cons:
1. Emotional Toll: Dealing with individuals facing emotional challenges can be emotionally taxing for art therapists.
2. Specialized Training: Art therapists require specialized training in both art and psychology, adding to the time and financial investment in education.
3. Limited Accessibility: Art therapy may not be readily accessible to

everyone due to factors like location, cost, or cultural stigma.

Architecture: The Art of Functional Design
Pros:
1. Functional Impact: Architects contribute to creating functional spaces that enhance the way people live, work, and interact.
2. Cultural Legacy: Iconic architectural designs can become cultural landmarks, leaving a lasting legacy.
3. Collaboration: Architects often collaborate with various professionals, including engineers and urban planners, enriching the creative process.

Cons:
1. Extensive Education: Becoming an architect requires extensive education and training, involving a significant time commitment.
2. Regulatory Challenges: Navigating building codes and regulations can be complex and adds an additional layer of challenge to architectural projects which can feel limiting.
3. Project Timelines: Architectural projects, especially large-scale ones, may have extended timelines, requiring patience and persistence.

Graphic and Digital Design: Navigating the Digital Landscape
Pros:
1. Versatility: Graphic and digital designers can work across various industries, from marketing to user experience design.
2. Dynamic Medium: The digital landscape allows for dynamic and interactive design, contributing to innovative storytelling.
3. Global Reach: Designers can reach a global audience through digital platforms, expanding the impact of their work.

Cons:
1. Fast-paced Changes: The digital design landscape evolves rapidly, requiring designers to stay updated on emerging trends and technologies.
2. Intellectual Property Concerns: Designers may face challenges related to intellectual property rights, especially in the online environment.
3. Potential for Repetition: Some design projects may limit creative freedom, as certain clients or industries may have specific requirements.

Curating and Art Management: Behind the Scenes of the Art World
Pros:

1. Cultural Influence: Curators and art managers shape cultural narratives, influencing the appreciation of art in society.
2. Networking Opportunities: This profession offers extensive networking opportunities, connecting individuals with artists, collectors, and other professionals.
3. Diverse Responsibilities: Art managers engage in diverse tasks, from exhibition planning to budget management, ensuring a varied and dynamic work environment.

Cons:
1. Logistical Challenges: Managing exhibitions involves intricate logistical details, from transportation to installation.
2. High Expectations: The success of exhibitions and institutions may be subject to high expectations, adding pressure to curators and art managers.
3. Balancing Commercial and Artistic Goals: Striking a balance between commercial success and artistic integrity can be challenging in the art management field.

Teaching and Mentoring: Sharing Your Passion with Others
Pros:
1. Impactful Contribution: Educators contribute to the development of future artists, making a meaningful impact on the art community.
2. Continuous Learning: Teaching involves continual learning, allowing educators to stay updated on artistic trends and theories.
3. Community Building: Teaching fosters the creation of a community of artists, encouraging collaboration and shared creativity.

Cons:
1. Administrative Responsibilities: Educators may face administrative duties that take time away from direct teaching and mentoring.
2. Varied Student Skill Levels: In a classroom setting, students may have diverse skill levels, requiring educators to tailor their approach to individual needs.
3. Institutional Constraints: Educational institutions may have constraints that limit creative freedom or require adherence to specific curricula.

The Ever-Expanding Artistic Horizon

As artists venture into these diverse realms, they navigate a landscape of both challenges and rewards. Each path offers a unique canvas for creative expression, and the decision to pursue a specific career should align with an individual's passions, values, and aspirations. Beyond the easel, the world of art-infused careers is vast and dynamic, continually inviting artists to redefine success and contribute to the ever-evolving narrative of art in society.

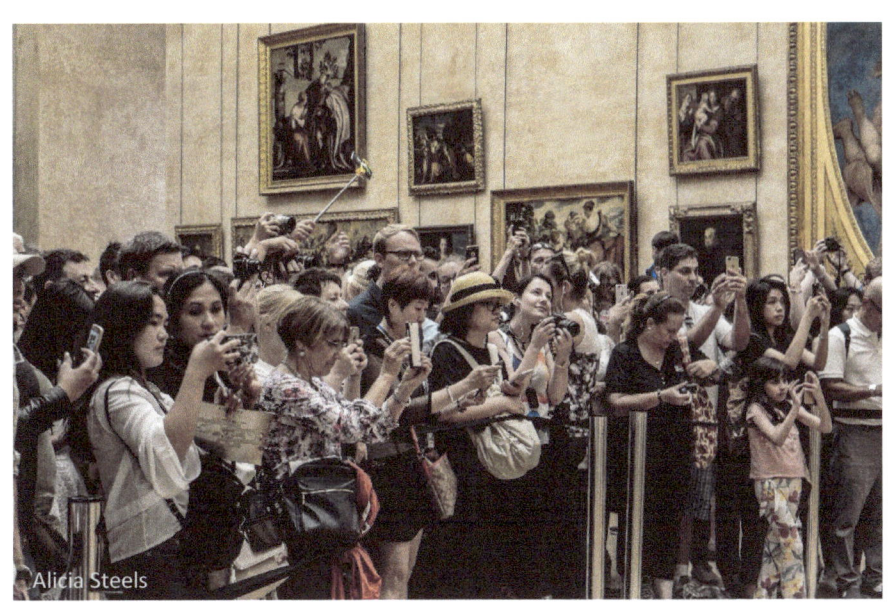
Alicia Steels

CHAPTER 11: TO CONCLUDE
ARTFUL FUTURES AWAIT

As we navigate the final strokes of this artistic narrative, it's time to step back, take stock, and face the blank canvas of the future with newfound insight. In this concluding chapter, we'll reflect on the pivotal lessons learned throughout this book, extend a dose of encouragement to those budding artists embarking on their journey, explore the significance of embracing both challenges and triumphs, and cast a discerning gaze forward to envision a sustainable and fulfilling career in the ever-evolving world of art.

Time for Reflection: What We've Learned

This book has been a roadmap through the labyrinth of turning artistic passion into a profession. From honing skills and crafting a compelling portfolio to navigating the digital realm and delving into the diverse path's art can take, we've covered it all. But beyond the tangible steps lies a deeper understanding: art is not just about creation; it's a dance with the unexpected, a journey of constant evolution.

We've unravelled the myth of the "starving artist," debunked misconceptions, and explored the myriad possibilities that extend beyond traditional easels. Each chapter was a brushstroke contributing to a bigger picture - the blueprint for a sustainable and impactful artistic career.

Looking Ahead: A Sustainable Career in Art

The future of your artistic career is a canvas waiting to be filled. It's not just about surviving; it's about thriving in a landscape that demands both creativity and practicality. As you look ahead, consider these guiding principles for cultivating a sustainable career in art:

1. Diversify Your Artistic Portfolio:
- Experiment with various mediums, styles, and themes.
- Your versatility is your strength; let it shine through your diverse body of work.

2. Cultivate a Robust Online Presence:
- Your online presence is your digital storefront. Invest in a professional website and leverage social media platforms.
- Engage with your audience, share your process, and let your personality shine through your digital persona.

3. Network Strategically:
- Networking isn't just about collecting business cards; it's about building genuine connections.
- Attend exhibitions, collaborate with fellow artists, and foster relationships that extend beyond the canvas.

4. Adaptability is Non-Negotiable:
- The art world evolves rapidly. Stay adaptable, embrace new technologies, and be open to unconventional approaches.
- Your ability to adapt ensures your relevance in an ever-changing creative landscape.

5. Balance Passion with Practicality:
- Passion fuels your creativity, but practicality sustains your career.
- Understand the business side of art - pricing, contracts, and marketing. A balanced approach is key to longevity.

6. Continuous Learning is Your Superpower:
- The pursuit of knowledge is a never-ending journey. Enrol in workshops, take online courses, and engage with the artistic community.

- Stagnation is the enemy of progress; let curiosity be your guide.

Encouragement for Aspiring Artists

To the artists standing at the precipice of their creative endeavours, teetering on the edge between uncertainty and ambition, here's the unfiltered truth: this path isn't for the faint of heart. It's riddled with doubt, rejection, and the perpetual fear of the unknown. Yet, in this chaos lies the beauty of creation, the uncharted territory where your unique voice can echo.

Embrace the struggle, for it is in the struggle that resilience is forged. It's okay to question, to falter, and to feel the weight of uncertainty. These are not signs of weakness; they are the birth pangs of artistic growth. Let this be your permission to be imperfect, to experiment boldly, and to define success on your terms.

Embrace the challenges not as impediments but as catalysts for growth. The frustration of a blank canvas or the rejection of a piece is not a sign to retreat but a signal to innovate. It's in these moments of friction that the most profound breakthroughs occur.

Triumphs, both big and small, are the rewards for navigating the challenges. Completing a body of work, landing an exhibition, or receiving recognition - these are not just markers of success; they are testaments to your dedication. Celebrate them. Savor the satisfaction of a finished piece, relish the impact your art has on others, and let these triumphs propel you forward.

To Conclude…

Artful futures don't just await; they demand your active participation. It's not about waiting for opportunities; it's about creating them. The canvas is in your hands, and the strokes you make today shape the narrative of tomorrow. So, go forth, create boldly, and let your artistic journey unfold with a fierce and unyielding determination. Artful futures await, and they are yours to claim.

Alexander Abbott is an experienced artist with a background in fine arts, digital art, and entrepreneurship. Through his book "Artful Ambitions: Your Guide to a Thriving Art Career," he aims to share industry secrets and practical advice to empower aspiring artists to achieve success in the art world.